JUV/E
QC
863.5
.W55
2004

WWOOD

MAY

2005

Chicago Public Library

Searching for stormy weather with a scie

D1313553

CHICAGO PUBLIC LIBRARY
WEST ENGLEWOOD BRANCH
1745 W. 63rd STREET
CHICAGO, IL 60636

I Like Science!

Searching for
STORMY
WEATHER
with a
Scientist

Judith Williams

Enslow Publishers, Inc.

40 Industrial Road
Box 398
Berkeley Heights, NJ 07922
USA

P.O. Box 38
Aldershot
Hants GU12 6BP
UK

http://www.enslow.com

Contents

Words to Know

blizzard (BLIZ urd)—Cold weather with snow and strong winds. There is so much blowing snow it is hard to see.

forecast (FOR cast)—A report that tells what the weather will be like.

hail (HAYL)—Small pieces of ice that fall like rain.

hurricane (HER ih cayn)—A large storm that starts on the ocean and can move on to land.

meteorologist (meet ee or AH loh jist)—A scientist who studies the weather.

severe (sa VEER) weather—Bad and sometimes unsafe weather.

tornado (tor NAY doh)—A strong twisting wind below a thunderstorm that touches the ground.

CHICAGO PUBLIC LIBRARY
WEST ENGLEWOOD BRANCH
1745 W. 63rd STREET
CHICAGO, IL 60636
R0403822081

What is weather?

Weather is sunny days, rainy nights, windy mornings, and snowy afternoons.

Scientists learn about weather to keep us safe. What an important job!

Meet meteorologist Harold Brooks.

He is a weather scientist.

He learns about severe weather, like strong winds, hail, and thunderstorms.

Why does this weather sometimes start
tornadoes? Where? When? These are
questions he asks about storms.

Meteorologists watch weather maps on computers. The maps show the changing weather. Is it wet? Is it windy or hot?

These answers help meteorologists make a forecast. The forecast tells us what the weather will be.

What is a weather watch?

Meteorologists see that severe weather, like hail, might happen where you live. Watch the sky! Is it getting dark?

It might be time for a weather warning.

What is a weather warning?

A weather warning tells us that severe weather has started. Be sure to go to a safe place.

hail on the ground

hail

Is there ever a snow watch or warning?

Yes. People need to be ready for lots of snow.

10

Sometimes the weather gets really cold and there are high winds and snow. This is called a **blizzard**.

Is there severe weather on the ocean?

Yes. Huge ocean storms in North America are called **hurricanes**.

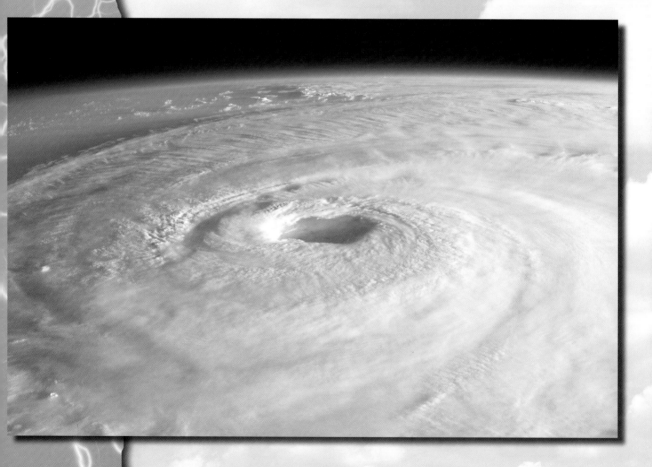

If a hurricane moves onto land, the wind can blow down buildings. Heavy rain and big waves can start floods.

Thunderstorms! They have rain, wind, thunder, and lightning. Sometimes hail falls with the rain.

Meteorologists watch carefully.
They look for clues that a tornado
could start.

1.

cool air

warm air

rain

1. Thunderstorms start when warm, wet air rises high into the sky. This makes clouds.

16

2. The wind under a storm cloud blows hard. The air on the ground moves slower. This makes the wind in between roll like a long tube.

fast wind

slow wind

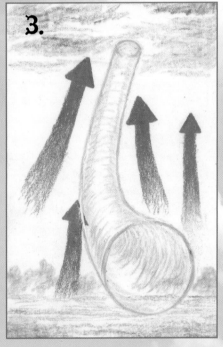

3. Sometimes the warm air lifts one end of the spinning tube up into the cloud.

4. As the wind, rain, and air around the tube touch the ground, a tornado can be formed.

How does meteorologist Harold learn about tornadoes?

He studies past storms. He puts these facts into a computer. The facts make a model.

The colors help show where storms might start.

This computer model helps Harold see how storms are going to move.

Models run like a computer game. They show why some storms start tornadoes. These facts help forecast new tornadoes around the world.

Early storm warnings are important.
By learning about severe weather,
scientists help save lives. Thank you,
meteorologist Harold, for watching the
weather for us.

You will need:

- ✔ empty plastic soda bottle with a lid
- ✔ warm water
- ✔ dishwashing soap
- ✔ glitter

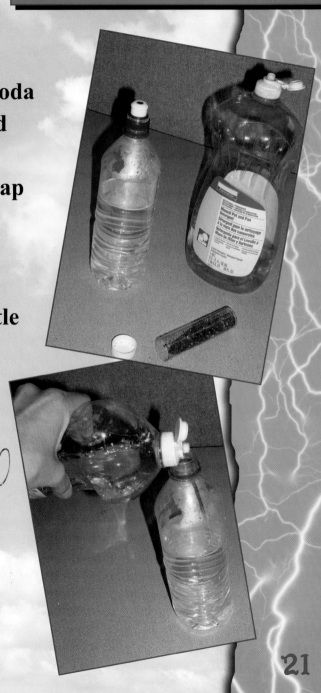

1. Fill a soda bottle halfway with warm water. Add a drop of dishwashing soap and a bit of glitter.

2. Put the top on tightly. Face a sunny window. Shake the bottle in circles many times.

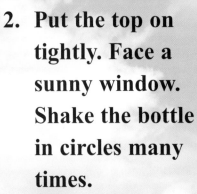

3. Hold the bottle up toward the sunny window. Do you see the twister? The wind of a tornado spins almost the same way.

Books

Berger, Melvin and Gilda. *Do Tornadoes Really Twist?* New York: Scholastic Inc., 2000.

De Saules, Janet, and Hazel Songhurst. *All About the Weather*. New York: Smithmark Publishers, 1997.

DeWitt, Lynda. *What Will the Weather Be?* New York: HarperCollins Publishers, 1991.

Herman, Gail. *Storm Chasers.* New York: Grosset & Dunlop, 1997.

Malam, John. *Wacky Weather*. New York: Simon & Schuster for Young Readers, 1998.

Web Sites

National Weather Service: Storm Prediction Center
<http://www.spc.noaa.gov>

National Severe Storms Laboratory
<http://www.nssl.noaa.gov>

Web Weather for Kids
<http://www.ucar.edu/educ_outreach/webweather/index.html>

Index

Series Literacy Consultant:
Allan A. De Fina, Ph.D.
Past President of the New Jersey Reading Association
Professor, Department of Literacy Education
New Jersey City University

Science Consultant:
Harold Brooks, Ph.D.
Meteorologist
NOAA/National Severe Storms Laboratory
Norman, Oklahoma

Note to Teachers and Parents: The I Like Science! series supports the National Science Education Standards for K–4 science, including content standards "Science as a human endeavor" and "Science as inquiry." The Words to Know section introduces subject-specific vocabulary, including pronunciation and definitions. Early readers may require help with these new words.

Copyright © 2004 by Enslow Publishers, Inc.

All rights reserved.

No part of this book may be reproduced by any means without the written permission of the publisher.

Library of Congress Cataloging-in-Publication Data

Williams, Judith (Judith A.)
    Searching for stormy weather with a scientist / Judith Williams.
        p. cm.— (I like science!)
    Summary: Briefly explains the work of meteorologists, scientists who study weather in order to warn people about storms.
    Includes index.
    ISBN 0-7660-2271-4 (hardcover)
    1. Meteorology—Juvenile literature. [1. Meteorology.]
I. Title. II. Series.
QC863.5.W55 2004
551.55—dc22

2003012826

Printed in the United States of America

10 9 8 7 6 5 4 3 2 1

To Our Readers: We have done our best to make sure all Internet Addresses in this book were active and appropriate when we went to press. However, the author and the publisher have no control over and assume no liability for the material available on those Internet sites or on other Web sites they may link to. Any comments or suggestions can be sent by e-mail to comments@enslow.com or to the address on the back cover.

Photo Credits: © David Cavagnaro/Visuals Unlimited, p. 7; © Jeff J. Daly/Visuals Unlimited, p. 9 (inset); © Charles A. Doswell III/Visuals Unlimited, pp. 14, 19; Enslow Publishers, Inc., pp. 21, 22; © Marc Epstein/Visuals Unlimited, p. 13; © Joseph L. Fontenot/Visuals Unlimited, p. 3 (top); © Carlyn Galati/Visuals Unlimited, p. 9; © Joe McDonald/Visuals Unlimited, pp. 10–11; NASA, p. 2 (center); NOAA, p. 12; NOAA Photo Library, NOAA Central Library; OAR/National Severe Storms Lab, p. 15; NSSL, pp. 4, 20; NOAA/Storm Prediction Center, p. 18; © Gene Rhoden/Visuals Unlimited, p. 5; © Mark A. Schneider/Visuals Unlimited, p. 8; © Michael W. Skrepnick, pp. 16, 17; © Tom Uhlman/Visuals Unlimited, p. 6; © Visuals Unlimited, p. 3 (bottom).

Cover Photo: © A & J Verkaik/CORBIS